WHY I LOVE YOU

THE LITTLE BOOK WITH A 'BIG' HEART

The Life Graduate Publishing Group

No part of this book may be scanned, reproduced or distributed in any printed or electronic form without the prior permission of the author or publisher.
Copyright - The Life Graduate Publishing Group 2021 - All Rights Reserved

★★★★★

We love to receive reviews from our customers. If you had the opportunity to provide a review we would greatly appreciate it. Thank you!

DEAR..

I WROTE THIS BOOK JUST FOR YOU!

LOVE..

THIS BOOK IS WRITTEN ROM MY HEART. I CREATED IT FOR YOU BECAUSE.....

_____

_____

_____

_____

_____

_____

_____

_____

WHEN WE ARE APART, I REALLY MISS...

_____
_____
_____
_____
_____
_____

WHEN I CLOSE MY EYES AND I THINK OF YOU I SEE...

_____

_____

_____

_____

THESE ARE 3 THINGS YOU DO THAT ARE KIND AND THOUGHTFUL

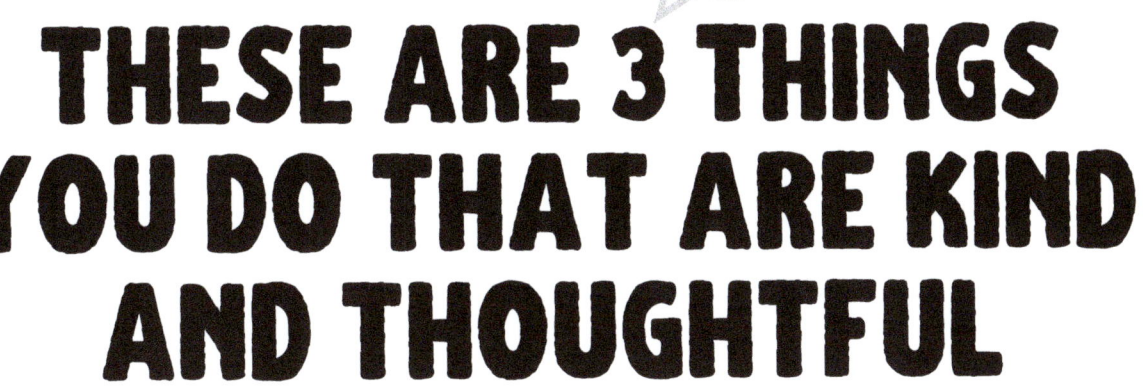

1. _____

   _____

2. _____

   _____

3. _____

   _____

I LOVE IT WHEN YOU...

THIS IS SOMEWHERE I LOVE TO VISIT WITH YOU.

I WOULD LIKE TO SAY THANK YOU FOR....

I'VE NEVER SAID THIS TO YOU BEFORE, BUT I LOVE IT WHEN YOU...

_____

_____

_____

BECAUSE...

_____

_____

_____

_____

_____

YOU LOVE IT WHEN I....

11

YOU MAKE ME LAUGH WHEN....

YOU MAKE ME CRY WHEN....

YOU MAKE ME SMILE WHEN....

IF I COULD TAKE YOU ANYWHERE IN THE WORLD, WE WOULD VISIT..

BOARDING PASS SEAT: **1A**

DEPARTING LOCATION

ARRIVING LOCATION

WE WOULD VISIT THIS LOCATION BECAUSE

_____

_____

_____

THIS WAS SOMETHING
SPECIAL THAT YOU DID
FOR ME THAT I WILL
NEVER FORGET.....

THIS IS SOMETHING SPECIAL THAT YOU SAID TO ME...

YOU CAN DO THIS BETTER THAN ANYONE ELSE!

WHEN I HEAR YOUR VOICE, IT MAKES ME FEEL

 **BECAUSE....**

I WISH THAT ONE DAY WE CAN DO THIS...

I THINK YOUR SPECIAL 'SUPER-POWER' IS.....

YOU DIDN'T KNOW THIS BUT I...

THESE ARE 3 WORDS THAT BEST DESCRIBE YOU.

1. _____

2. _____

3. _____

SPECIAL MOMENTS or MEMORIES

Add other special photo's or details here

SPECIAL MOMENTS or MEMORIES

Add other special photo's or details here ↙

SPECIAL MOMENTS or MEMORIES

Add other special photo's or details here

SPECIAL MOMENTS or MEMORIES

Add other special photo's or details here

I WROTE THIS BOOK BECAUSE I LOVE YOU!

Kisses and Hugs

THIS HAS BEEN MY SPECIAL GIFT FOR YOU.

I HOPE YOU LIKE IT!

A sample of other books created by The Life Graduate Publishing Group

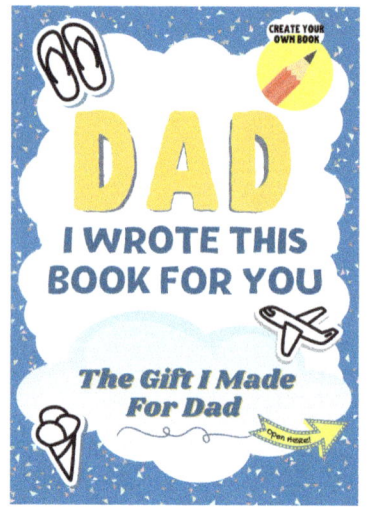
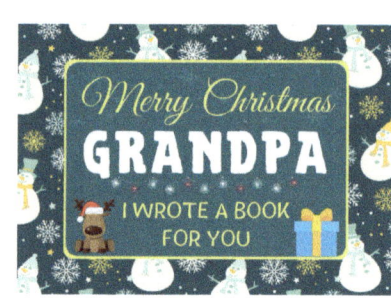
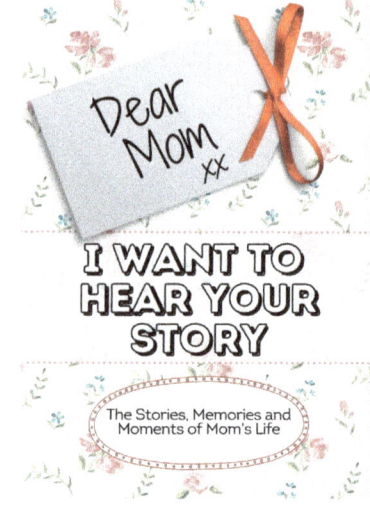

www.thelifegraduate.com/bookstore

www.ingramcontent.com/pod-product-compliance
Ingram Content Group UK Ltd.
Pitfield, Milton Keynes, MK11 3LW, UK
UKHW052120230426
12049UKWH00009BA/137